CRAFTY
T-Shirts

Petra Boase

Gareth Stevens Publishing
MILWAUKEE

This book is dedicated to Lucy.

The original publishers would like to thank the following children for modeling for this book: Nana Addae, Kristina Chase, Charlie Coulson, Reece Johnson, Alex Lindblom-Smith, Sophie Lindblom-Smith, Imran Miah, Lucy Nightingale, Tom Swaine Jameson, and Sophie Viner. Thanks also to their parents and Walnut Tree Walk Primary School.

For a free color catalog describing Gareth Stevens' list of high-quality books and multimedia programs, call 1-800-542-2595 (USA) or 1-800-461-9120 (Canada). Gareth Stevens Publishing's Fax: (414) 225-0377.

Library of Congress Cataloging-in-Publication Data

Boase, Petra.
    Crafty T-shirts / by Petra Boase.
      p. cm. — (Crafty kids)
    Includes bibliographical references and index.
    Summary: Instructions for decorating T-shirts with fabric paints, threads, and other materials.
    ISBN 0-8368-2483-0 (lib. bdg.)
    1. Textile painting—Juvenile literature. 2. T-shirts—Juvenile literature. [1. T-shirts. 2. Textile crafts. 3. Handicraft.] I. Title. II. Series.
TT851.B63   1999
746.6'0432—dc21   99-22879

This North American edition first published in 1999 by
Gareth Stevens Publishing
1555 North RiverCenter Drive, Suite 201
Milwaukee, WI 53212 USA

Original edition © 1997 by Anness Publishing Limited. First published in 1997 by Lorenz Books, an imprint of Anness Publishing Limited, New York, New York. This U.S. edition © 1999 by Gareth Stevens, Inc. Additional end matter © 1999 by Gareth Stevens, Inc.

Editor: Lyn Coutts
Photographer: John Freeman
Designer: Caroline Grimshaw
Gareth Stevens series editor: Dorothy L. Gibbs
Editorial assistant: Diane Laska

Printed in Mexico

1 2 3 4 5 6 7 8 9 03 02 01 00 99

Introduction

Painting and decorating T-shirts is fun and very easy to do. In no time at all, you will be creating stylish and wacky T-shirts for yourself, friends, and family.

This book shows you how to prepare T-shirts for painting and decorating, as well as how to use different types of fabric paints to achieve stunning effects. It is bursting with ideas. You will find T-shirt designs for sports fans, space enthusiasts, and animal lovers. There are even designs for birthday gifts and costume parties. Most of the projects are simple. A few are more difficult and use special techniques.

Once you have painted your first T-shirt, there will be no stopping you. You will be painting sweatshirts, leggings, and even fabrics for your bedroom. So get started and have fun!

Petra Boase

Contents

Materials

EMBROIDERY NEEDLE
The large eye in this needle makes it easy to thread with embroidery floss.

EMBROIDERY FLOSS
A strong, thick, multi-stranded thread that comes in lots of bright colors and is used for decorative stitching.

FABRIC CHALK
This special white chalk is used to draw outlines on dark-colored T-shirts.

FABRIC GLUE AND BRUSH
This kind of glue will stick pieces of fabric together. Always use a special brush to apply fabric glue.

FABRIC MARKER
This marker looks like a normal felt-tip pen, but it is designed to be used on fabrics.

FABRIC PAINTS
When these paints are applied to fabrics, they will not wash out. Always follow the instructions on the containers.

FELT
This material is easy to cut and will not fray. It can be bought at fabric stores or craft shops.

FLUORESCENT FABRIC PAINTS
Under ultraviolet light, these paints will glow. They come in many bright colors.

GLITTER
This special glitter is attached to fabrics with fabric glue. The pieces are very tiny, so be careful.

GLITTER FABRIC PAINTS
These sparkly paints come in tubes or plastic squeeze bottles. Always follow the instructions on the containers.

HAIR DRYER
You will need a hair dryer with a low heat setting to dry puffy fabric paints.

BARRETTES
To complete the "Hairdo Suzie" project, you will need two plastic barrettes.

NEWSPAPER
Protect your work surface by covering it with newspaper.

PAINTBRUSHES
You will need fine, medium, and thick paintbrushes. Always wash the brushes before changing paint colors.

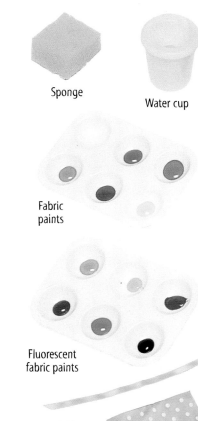

Sponge

Water cup

Fabric paints

Fluorescent fabric paints

Ribbons

PEARL FABRIC PAINTS
These paints dry to a special sheen. They come in plastic squeeze bottles.

PUFFY FABRIC PAINTS
When dried with a hair dryer, these paints puff up. They come in plastic squeeze bottles. Always follow the instructions on the containers.

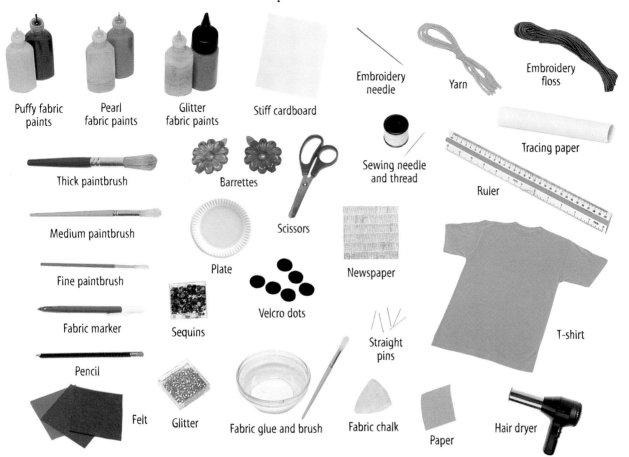

Puffy fabric paints

Pearl fabric paints

Glitter fabric paints

Stiff cardboard

Embroidery needle

Yarn

Embroidery floss

Thick paintbrush

Barrettes

Scissors

Sewing needle and thread

Tracing paper

Ruler

Medium paintbrush

Fine paintbrush

Plate

Newspaper

Fabric marker

Sequins

Velcro dots

Pencil

Straight pins

T-shirt

Felt

Glitter

Fabric glue and brush

Fabric chalk

Paper

Hair dryer

SEQUINS
These colorful, jewel-like decorations can be attached to fabrics with fabric glue.

SPONGE
An inexpensive sponge dipped in fabric paint and pressed onto a T-shirt makes an interesting texture. A sponge can also be used for stenciling.

VELCRO DOTS
These dots have a texture that makes them stick to each other when pressed together.

STIFF CARDBOARD
Cardboard is inserted into the body and sleeves of a T-shirt to keep fabric paints from seeping through. Cardboard is also used to make stencils.

TRACING PAPER
You can see through this special paper. It is used to trace stencils and templates. You can buy it at a stationery store.

T-SHIRT
For each project in this book, you will need a cotton T-shirt. There are designs for both short- and long-sleeved styles.

Preparing the T-shirt

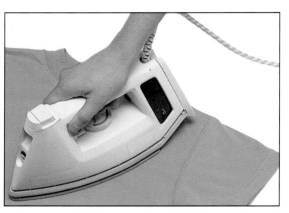

1 If you are using a new T-shirt, it is a good idea to wash and rinse it to remove excess dye. When the T-shirt is dry, ask an adult to iron it to smooth out creases.

2 To prevent fabric paints from seeping through the T-shirt, insert pieces of stiff cardboard into the body and sleeves. The cardboard should fit snugly.

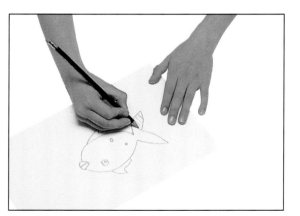

3 Practice drawing your design on a piece of paper before drawing it on the T-shirt. Fabric marker, like fabric paints, cannot be washed out.

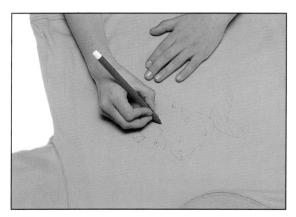

4 When you are happy with your design, draw it on the T-shirt. Use a fabric marker on light-colored T-shirts. Use fabric chalk on dark-colored T-shirts.

Painting Tips

1 If you have only a few colors of fabric paints, combine them to make other colors. For example, **yellow + blue = green**; **yellow + red = orange**; **red + blue = purple**.

2 If you need a large quantity of a color, it is best to mix it in a cup or a small bowl. Add water to fabric paints to make them go further.

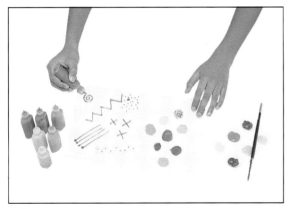

3 Before painting the T-shirt, try out techniques and colors on a piece of fabric. Practice is especially important when using fabric paints in squeeze bottles.

4 Puffy paints puff up only when they are dried with a hair dryer set on low heat. Before drying other fabric paints this way, read the instructions on the paint containers.

Making a Template

1 Cover the template pattern with a sheet of tracing paper. Use masking tape to hold the tracing paper in place. Trace the outline of the pattern with a lead pencil.

2 Remove the tracing paper and turn it facedown on a clean sheet of paper. Draw lots of fine pencil lines over the back of the traced outline.

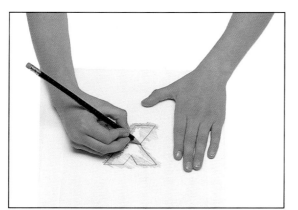

3 With the traced outline faceup, place the tracing paper on a piece of thin cardboard. Draw over the outline. The pattern will be transferred onto the cardboard.

4 To make the template, cut out the cardboard pattern. Place the template on the T-shirt and draw around it with a marker. Save the template to use again.

Template Patterns

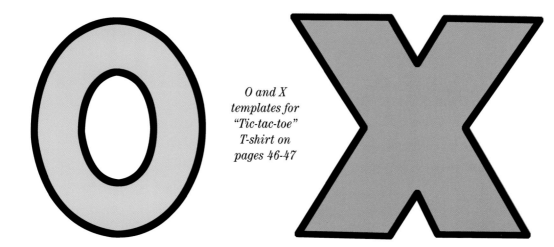

Dog template for "Muddy Puppy"
T-shirt on pages 16-17

O and X
templates for
"Tic-tac-toe"
T-shirt on
pages 46-47

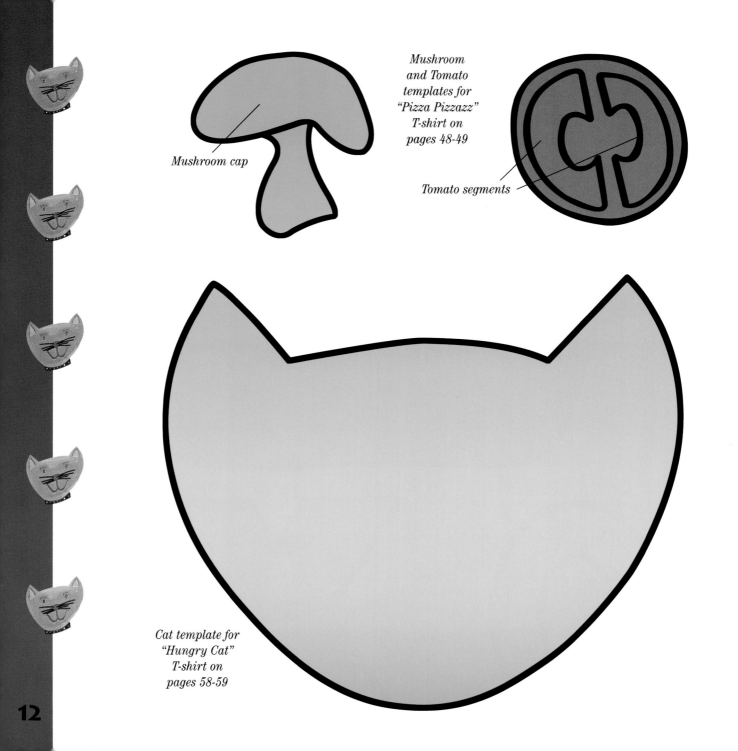

Mushroom and Tomato templates for "Pizza Pizzazz" T-shirt on pages 48-49

Mushroom cap

Tomato segments

Cat template for "Hungry Cat" T-shirt on pages 58-59

12

Making a Stencil

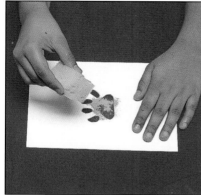

1 Follow steps 1 through 3 on page 10 to make a template outline on cardboard. Snip into the middle of the outline and cut out the inside to create a stencil.

2 Position the stencil on the T-shirt. Lightly press a dry sponge into fabric paint. Then dab the sponge over the stencil until the cut-out area is painted.

3 Carefully lift the stencil off the T-shirt. Before using the stencil again, be sure to wipe off any blobs of paint on the back side of it.

STENCILS

Fish skeleton stencil for "Hungry Cat" T-shirt on pages 58-59

Paw-print stencil for "Muddy Puppy" T-shirt on pages 16-17

Tutti-Frutti

The fruit on this T-shirt looks good enough to eat! To make it look more realistic, paint areas of shadow and light. Add texture with dots of pearl fabric paints and felt leaves.

YOU WILL NEED
- Large piece of cardboard
- Short-sleeved T-shirt
- Fabric marker
- Cup of water
- Fabric paints (yellow, red, pink, crimson)
- Thick paintbrush
- Pearl fabric paints (yellow, pink)
- Green felt
- Scissors
- Fabric glue and brush

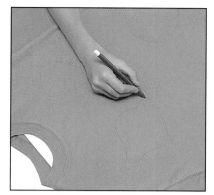

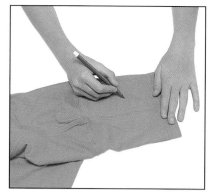

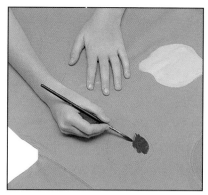

1 Place cardboard inside the body of the T-shirt. Use the fabric marker to draw the outlines of a lemon, an orange, a strawberry, and a raspberry on the front of the T-shirt.

2 Lay one sleeve out flat with the seam on the bottom. Insert cardboard into the sleeve. Use the fabric marker to draw a piece of fruit on the sleeve. Repeat this step with the other sleeve.

3 Paint the fruit on the front of the T-shirt. To make orange fabric paint, combine red and yellow. Let the paint dry on the front of the T-shirt before painting the fruit on the sleeves.

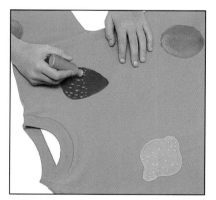

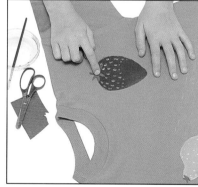

4 To add texture to the orange, strawberry, and lemon, make dots on them using yellow and pink pearl fabric paints. Let this paint dry before adding texture to the fruit on the sleeves.

5 Use the fabric marker to draw the outlines of leaves on the green felt. Cut out the leaves and attach them to the fruit with fabric glue. Let the glue dry before trying on your Tutti-Frutti T-shirt.

15

Muddy Puppy

Oh, no! Someone let a puppy with muddy paws walk all over this T-shirt! Surely such a bad puppy does not deserve a big, juicy bone! To keep the puppy from getting everything in the house muddy, you can give it a fancy pair of socks to wear.

YOU WILL NEED

- 2 pieces of cardboard
- Short-sleeved, light-colored T-shirt
- Pencil
- Tracing paper
- Scissors
- Fabric marker
- Cup of water
- Fabric paints (brown, black, white, turquoise, red, light blue, yellow)
- Fine and thick paintbrushes
- Narrow yellow ribbon
- Fabric glue and brush
- Sponge

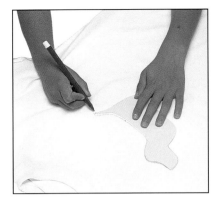

1 Place pieces of cardboard inside the body and sleeves of the T-shirt. Make the dog template on page 11. Place the template on the front of the T-shirt and use the fabric marker to draw around it.

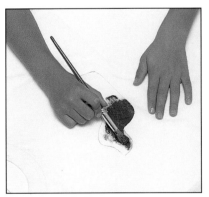

2 Use the thick paintbrush to paint the dog brown. If you do not have brown paint, make some by combining blue, red, and yellow. To make light and dark shades of brown, add white or black. Let the paint dry before starting the next step.

16

3 Use the fine paintbrush to paint black spots on the dog's body. Also use black paint for its ear, tail, shoes, and bone. Then, paint features on its face, decorate its socks and shoes, and paint a collar.

4 When the paint is completely dry, tie the piece of ribbon into a small bow and trim the ends. Attach the bow to the collar with fabric glue. Hold the bow in position until the glue is dry.

5 Make the paw-print stencil on page 13 and cut out the stencil as shown above. Turn the T-shirt over so the back is facing you. Make sure the pieces of cardboard are still in position inside the T-shirt.

6 Place the paw-print stencil on the T-shirt. Holding the stencil securely in position, dab light and dark brown fabric paint over it with a sponge. Lift off the stencil and repeat this step until the back of the T-shirt is full of muddy paw prints.

Crazy Spiral

For someone new to fabric painting, this wacky T-shirt is a cinch to make. Draw the outline of the spiral as large as you can to make it easy to paint and decorate. You can add smaller spirals to the design or paint a spiral on the back of the T-shirt, too.

YOU WILL NEED

- Large piece of cardboard
- Short-sleeved T-shirt
- Fabric marker
- Cup of water
- Fabric paints (black, orange, yellow, light blue, green)
- Fine, medium, and thick paintbrushes
- Pearl fabric paints (yellow, orange, purple)
- Glitter fabric paints (green, purple)

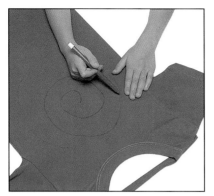

1 Place pieces of cardboard inside the body and sleeves of the T-shirt. Use the fabric marker to draw a large, curly spiral on the front of the T-shirt.

2 Use the thick paintbrush to paint the spiral with black fabric paint. Let the black paint dry thoroughly before you start decorating the spiral.

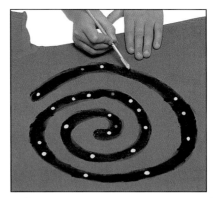

3 Use the medium paintbrush to decorate the spiral with dots of orange, yellow, light blue, and green fabric paints. Let the paints dry thoroughly.

4 Use yellow pearl fabric paint to draw circles around some of the dots. Outline the spiral with orange and purple pearl fabric paints. Be sure these paints are dry before adding the final touches.

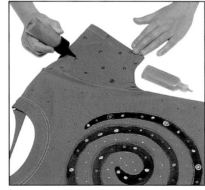

5 To finish the T-shirt, make dots inside the spiral with yellow pearl fabric paint. Then cover the front of the T-shirt with dots of green glitter fabric paint and dot the sleeves with purple glitter fabric paint.

Swirly Spots and Dots

This T-shirt is the perfect one to wear when you are out with your friends for a day of wild adventures. The design is simple to draw, and you can use as many or as few colors as you like. It is important to let the circles of fabric paint dry thoroughly before decorating them with puffy and glitter fabric paints.

YOU WILL NEED

- Large piece of cardboard
- Short-sleeved T-shirt
- Fabric marker
- Cup of water
- Medium paintbrush
- Fabric paints (red, black, dark and light pink, blue, white)
- Puffy fabric paints (purple, red, yellow, orange, blue)
- Hair dryer
- Glitter fabric paint (silver)

1 Place pieces of cardboard inside the body and sleeves of the T-shirt. Use the fabric marker to draw large circles on the front of the T-shirt. Draw circles on both sleeves, too.

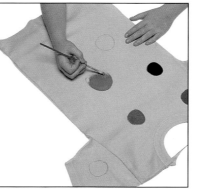

2 Use the medium paintbrush to paint the circles with different colors of fabric paints. Remember to wash the brush before you change colors. Let the paints dry thoroughly before decorating the circles.

3 Use purple, red, yellow, orange, and blue puffy fabric paints to decorate some of the circles with swirls, lines, dots, and spots. To make the puffy fabric paints puff up, dry them with the hair dryer.

HANDY HINT

When using puffy or glitter fabric paints in squeeze bottles, always keep the nozzle moving smoothly and evenly over your designs. If the nozzle stays in one place too long, the paint will form blobs.

4 To make your T-shirt even more dazzling, decorate the remaining circles with silver glitter fabric paint. You can also add glitter fabric paint to the circles already decorated with puffy fabric paints.

Bug Collector

Eek! Don't look now, but spiders and insects are crawling all over you. The Bug Collector T-shirt is not for the squeamish — it is for enthusiastic critter collectors who want to bug their friends and families. You can invent your own creatures or, even better, copy them from real life!

YOU WILL NEED
- Large piece of cardboard
- Long-sleeved T-shirt
- Fabric marker
- Cup of water
- Fabric paints (black, red)
- Fine and medium paintbrushes
- Black fabric paint or pearl fabric paint in a squeeze bottle

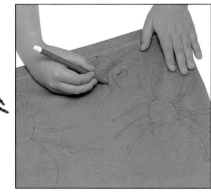

1 Place pieces of cardboard inside the body and sleeves of the T-shirt. Use the fabric marker to draw three large spiders on the front of the T-shirt. Draw two or three spiders on each sleeve.

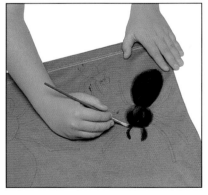

2 Use the medium paintbrush and black fabric paint to paint the spiders' heads, bodies, and fangs. Use the fine brush to paint their jointed legs. Wash the brush, then paint the spiders' eyes red.

3 Dip a finger into black fabric paint and press it onto the T-shirt to make the body and head of a small insect. Repeat this step until the front of the T-shirt is full of bugs. Let the paint dry.

HANDY HINT

To make repeated designs, such
as the small insects, you could make a
stamp from half of a potato. Carve the
insect's shape into the cut surface of
the potato with a blunt pencil. Ask an
adult to cut away the potato from
around the shape with a sharp knife.
Dip the stamp into fabric paint and
press it onto the T-shirt.

4 Use black fabric paint or pearl
fabric paint in a squeeze bottle
to paint legs on the small insects.
Let the paint dry thoroughly. Really
eager bug collectors can paint even
more bugs on the back of the T-shirt.

Cactus Flower

This cactus is on a yellow T-shirt because cacti grow in deserts. Even though rain rarely falls in a desert, a cactus can live for more than 100 years! Without leaves, it can hold in moisture longer, and it has prickly spines to keep animals from eating its juicy trunk. When it does rain in the desert, cacti burst into bloom.

1 Place pieces of cardboard into the body and sleeves of the T-shirt. Use the fabric marker to draw a flowering cactus in a pot on the front of the T-shirt. Draw a decorative border around the pot.

2 Use the fabric marker to draw zigzag patterns along the bottom of the T-shirt and around the collar and the edges of the sleeves. Use the medium paintbrush to paint the zigzag pattern red and blue.

3 Paint the pot red and the flower pink, and paint the border around the pot blue. Paint the cactus unevenly with light and dark green fabric paints. To make light green paint, add yellow to dark green.

4 Let the fabric paints dry. Then, thread the needle with embroidery floss and tie a knot at the end. Push the needle and thread in and out of the front of the T-shirt to make large stitches across the cactus. These stitches are the cactus's prickly spines. Knot the thread to secure the stitches.

HANDY HINT

Before decorating the back of a T-shirt, the paint on the front must be completely dry. You can often speed up the drying time by using a hair dryer, but always check the instructions on the fabric paint containers first. When you turn the T-shirt over, make sure the pieces of cardboard are still in position.

Space Trekker

This T-shirt goes where no other T-shirt has gone before. Its fluorescent yellow afterburners will be seen by alien beings in all the far-flung galaxies. But all space trekkers should make sure they know how to get back to Planet Earth!

YOU WILL NEED
- Large piece of cardboard
- Short-sleeved black T-shirt
- Fabric chalk
- Cup of water
- Fabric paints (dark and light blue, black, red, fluorescent yellow, silver)
- Medium and thick paintbrushes
- Pearl fabric paint (red)

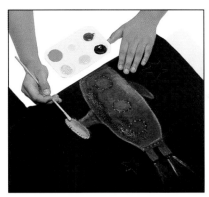

1 Place pieces of cardboard inside the body and sleeves of the T-shirt. Use the fabric chalk to draw the outlines of planets, stars, and a rocket. Draw only the end of the rocket and its thrusters on the front of the T-shirt.

2 Use the medium and thick paintbrushes to paint the rocket with dark blue, light blue, black, and red fabric paint. Use fluorescent yellow fabric paint for rivets and the glow of the afterburners. Paint the top of the rocket with silver fabric paint.

3 Paint the stars silver and use plain and fluorescent fabric paints for the planets. When these paints are dry, make a ring around each planet with red pearl fabric paint. Also use pearl fabric paint to add extra details to the rocket.

4 To make galaxies of stars, dip the thick paintbrush in fluorescent yellow fabric paint, then flick the brush at the T-shirt to splatter droplets of paint all over it. Repeat this step until the T-shirt glows with galaxies. Let the paint dry thoroughly.

5 Turn the T-shirt over, making sure the pieces of cardboard are still in position. Use the fabric chalk to draw the front of the rocket so it lines up with the back section on the front of the T-shirt. Paint and decorate the rocket as in step 2 and add galaxies of stars.

Sea Life Fantasy

When you look at this T-shirt, you can almost smell the salty air, hear the crash of the waves, and see schools of brightly colored fish darting around in a pale blue ocean. This design has only two kinds of marine life, but you can add crabs, shells, coral, and bright green seaweed.

YOU WILL NEED

- Large piece of cardboard
- Short-sleeved blue T-shirt
- Fabric marker
- Cup of water
- Fabric paints (light and dark blue, yellow, pink, red, black)
- Fine and thick paintbrushes

1 Place the piece of cardboard inside the body of the T-shirt. Use the fabric marker to draw the outlines of fish, starfish, and waves on the front of the T-shirt.

2 Use the thick paintbrush to paint the waves with light and dark blue fabric paints. Do not worry about spreading the paint evenly — uneven texture looks more realistic.

3 Paint the fish with blue, green, pink, and red fabric paints. Make green paint by mixing yellow and blue. Use the fine paintbrush to paint the fish's lips and eyes and the black bubbles coming from their mouths. Paint the starfish orange. Make orange paint by mixing red and yellow.

4 Let the paint on the front of the T-shirt dry thoroughly. Then turn the T-shirt over, making sure the cardboard stays in position. Use the fabric marker to continue the wave pattern and draw another fish on the back of the T-shirt.

5 Use the thick paintbrush to paint the waves with light and dark blue fabric paints. Wash the brush, then paint the fish pink with yellow spots. Paint features on the fish's face and bubbles coming from its mouth.

Team-shirt

If you can slam-dunk or kick a goal, then this is the T-shirt for you. Why not get together with some friends and start a basketball or soccer team? You can each have a different number, and you can choose your own team colors.

YOU WILL NEED
- Large piece of cardboard
- Short-sleeved T-shirt
- Fabric marker
- Cup of water
- Fabric paints (red, black)
- Medium and thick paintbrushes

1 Place pieces of cardboard inside the body and sleeves of the T-shirt. Use the fabric marker to draw the outline of the number 7 on the front. Draw a band along the edge of each sleeve front.

2 Use the thick paintbrush to fill in the outline of the number with red fabric paint. Try to spread the paint evenly and smoothly. Let the paint dry thoroughly before starting the next step.

3 Use the medium paintbrush to paint a narrow line around the number with black fabric paint. (You can use different colors to match your favorite team if you like.) Let the paint dry thoroughly.

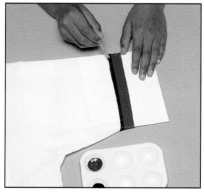

4 Wash the thick paintbrush, then use it to fill in the band on each sleeve with red fabric paint. When the red paint is dry, use the medium paintbrush to paint a narrow black line along the edge of the band.

5 Paint the ribbing around the neck of the T-shirt with black fabric paint. When the black paint is dry, paint a narrow red line around the ribbing. When the red paint is completely dry, turn the T-shirt over and repeat steps 1 through 5.

HANDY HINT
Use a ruler to make the outlines for the number and the sleeve bands straight.

Hawaiian Dancer

Aloha! Welcome to a tropical luau. "Luau" is the Hawaiian word for party, and the traditional dress for a luau dancer is a grass skirt and a lei of flowers around the neck. Wear some flowers in your hair and around your wrist and you will be ready to do the hula!

YOU WILL NEED

- Large piece of cardboard
- Long, sleeveless, light pink T-shirt
- Fabric marker
- Cup of water
- Fabric paints (yellow, pink, orange, red, white, green)
- Fine and thick paintbrushes

1 Place a piece of cardboard inside the body of the T-shirt. Use the fabric marker to draw the outlines of a flower lei, a belly button, and a grass skirt on the front of the T-shirt.

2 Use the fine paintbrush to paint the flowers of the lei with yellow, pink, orange, and red fabric paints. Add white paint to these colors to make lighter shades. Let the paint dry thoroughly.

3 Use the thick paintbrush to paint the grass skirt with different shades of green fabric paint. To make different shades of green paint, add yellow or white.

4 Use the fine paintbrush and pink fabric paint to make a belly button. When the fabric paint is completely dry, turn the T-shirt over. Make sure the cardboard stays in position.

5 Use the fabric marker to draw the outline of the lei and the grass skirt on the back of the T-shirt. Paint these items as in step 2. When the paint is dry, you are ready to hula!

Bones, the Skeleton

This spooky T-shirt is perfect for a Halloween costume party. All you need to complete this haunting outfit is a tight-fitting black cap, black leggings, and a pair of black gloves. To make your face look like a skull, cover it with white face paint or talcum powder and wear some black eye shadow.

YOU WILL NEED

- Large piece of cardboard
- Long-sleeved black T-shirt
- Fabric chalk
- Cup of water
- Fabric paint (white)
- Thick paintbrush

1 Place pieces of cardboard inside the body and sleeves of the T-shirt. Use the fabric chalk to draw the outlines of the shoulder blades, rib cage, spine, and hips.

2 Also use the fabric chalk to draw the outlines of the upper and lower arm bones on the front of each sleeve. The arm bones should be long and thick.

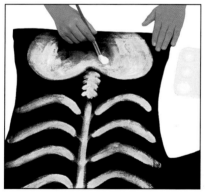

3 Use the thick paintbrush to paint the bones on the front of the T-shirt with white fabric paint. To make them really white, use two coats. Let the paint dry between coats.

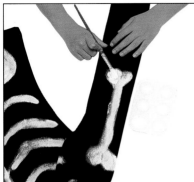

4 Paint the arm bones on both sleeves with two coats of white fabric paint. Let the paint dry thoroughly between coats. All you have to do now is wait for a full moon!

HANDY HINT

To keep the T-shirt from moving around while you are drawing outlines or painting your design on it, attach the T-shirt to your work surface with masking tape.

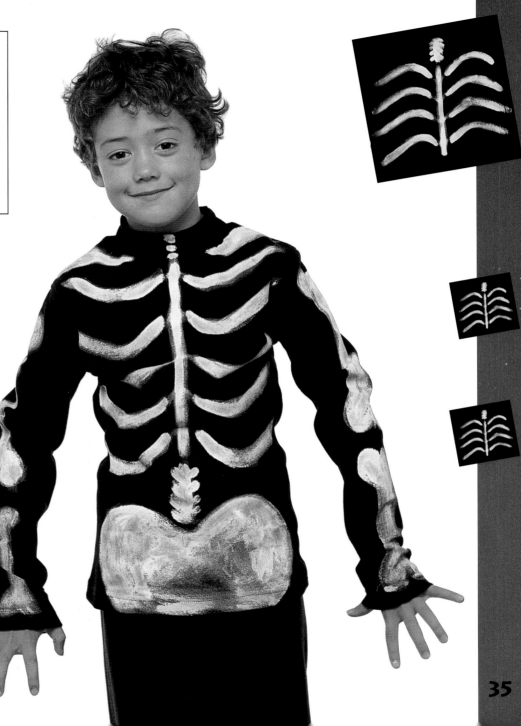

Pockets of Fun

When you wear this clever T-shirt, you will no longer lose or leave at home all your favorite odds and ends. You can even use one of the pockets to keep your allowance safe! Why not make a matching T-shirt for your best friend?

YOU WILL NEED

- Scissors
- Orange, lavender, green, and blue felt
- Fabric glue and brush
- Short-sleeved T-shirt
- Straight pins
- Embroidery needle
- Yellow, orange, and green embroidery floss
- Fabric marker
- Large piece of cardboard
- Cup of water
- Fabric paints (light blue, pink, yellow, orange, red, gold)
- Medium paintbrush

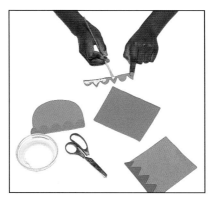

1 Cut three pockets and three decorative strips from the orange, lavender, green, and blue felt. Each decorative strip must be long enough to fit across the top edge of a pocket. Attach a strip to the top of each pocket with fabric glue.

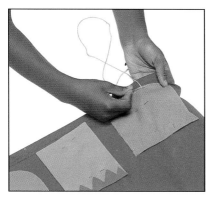

2 Pin the pockets along the bottom of the T-shirt. Thread the needle with embroidery floss and tie a knot in the end. Using a color of floss that is different than the color of the pocket, make big stitches to sew each pocket to the front of the T-shirt.

3 Use the fabric marker to draw the outlines of candy, coins, and dice just above each pocket. Some other items you could draw above the pockets are: pencils, erasers, sunglasses, jewelry, small toys, lipstick, and barrettes.

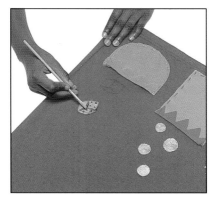

4 Place a piece of cardboard inside the body of the T-shirt. Paint the candy and dice with bright colors. Use gold fabric paint for the coins. When the paint is completely dry, put on your T-shirt and fill its pockets with all your treasures!

HANDY HINT

Place a piece of cardboard inside the body of the T-shirt when you sew on the pockets to avoid accidentally sewing the front and the back of the T-shirt together.

Modern Artist

Modern art has never been so much fun or so easy. To make this colorful, paint-splattered T-shirt, you just have to flick a paintbrush loaded with watered-down fabric paint all over the T-shirt. Try not to splatter paint on walls, furniture — or members of your family; it could mean an early end to a promising artistic career!

YOU WILL NEED
- Newspaper
- Large piece of cardboard
- Short-sleeved T-shirt
- Cup of water
- Fabric paints (yellow, orange, red, green, blue)
- Thick paintbrush

1 Cover your work surface with newspaper. Place pieces of cardboard inside the body and sleeves of the T-shirt. Add a little water to the fabric paints to make them runny. Dip the thick paint-brush into yellow fabric paint and flick the paint onto the T-shirt.

2 Wash the brush thoroughly before changing paint colors. Dip the clean brush into orange fabric paint and flick the paint onto the T-shirt.

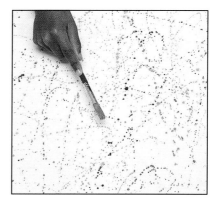

3 Repeat step 2 to add red, green, and blue fabric paints. You can flick as many colors as you like. Let the paint dry thoroughly before wearing your modern art.

HANDY HINT

When you want to make paints runny, add water a little at a time so you will not make them too runny. To splatter paint, start with the lightest color, then apply the darker colors. The last color you splatter on the T-shirt should be the darkest. To make a finer splatter, drag a plastic ruler across the bristles of an old toothbrush that has been dipped in watered-down fabric paint. Always pull the ruler toward you, unless you want to splatter yourself!

Razzle-Dazzler

When you wear this wild T-shirt, you will be the center of attention. Under ultraviolet light, the patterns positively glow in the dark. They have been painted with fluorescent fabric paints. If you want to have the ultimate razzle-dazzler, paint wild patterns on both the front and the back of the T-shirt.

YOU WILL NEED

- Large piece of cardboard
- Short-sleeved black T-shirt
- Fabric chalk
- Cup of water
- Medium paintbrush
- Fluorescent fabric paints (yellow, blue, pink, orange, green)
- Puffy fabric paints (orange, yellow, purple, red)
- Hair dryer

1 Place pieces of cardboard inside the body and sleeves of the T-shirt. Use the fabric chalk to draw the outlines of triangles, spirals, and zigzag patterns all over the front and the sleeves of the T-shirt.

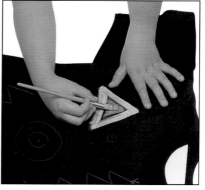

2 Use fluorescent yellow, blue, pink, orange, and green fabric paints to fill in the outlines. Combine these colors to make different colors. Let the fabric paint dry thoroughly before decorating the patterns.

3 Decorate your painted patterns with dots and squiggles of orange, yellow, purple, and red puffy paints. To make puffy fabric paints puff up, dry them with a hair dryer, on its coolest setting.

4 Use puffy fabric paints to decorate the bottom of the T-shirt with a zigzag pattern. Be sure to keep the hair dryer on its coolest setting when you dry the puffy paints.

Hairdo Suzie

How will you do Suzie's hair today? Will it be in braids, pigtails, or hanging straight? You can even do her hair in lots of fine braids with beads threaded onto the ends! Instead of barrettes, you could tie bows in Suzie's hair with brightly colored ribbons.

YOU WILL NEED

- Large piece of cardboard
- Short-sleeved T-shirt
- Fabric marker
- Cup of water
- Fine, medium, and thick paintbrushes

- Fabric paints (light and dark pink, white, red, blue, black)
- Scissors
- Yellow yarn
- Embroidery needle
- 2 barrettes

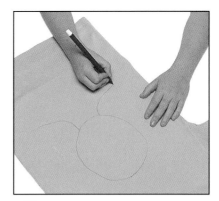

1 Place a piece of cardboard inside the body of the T-shirt. Use the fabric marker to draw the outline of a face and neck on the front of the T-shirt. Hairdo Suzie's head needs to be about 6 inches (15 centimeters) long.

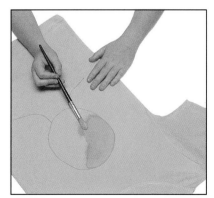

2 Use the thick paintbrush to fill in the outline with light pink fabric paint. Use dark pink fabric paint to make Suzie's rosy cheeks. Let the paint dry thoroughly before adding features to Suzie's face.

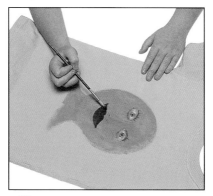

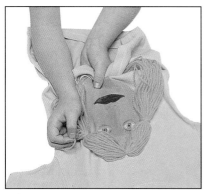

3 Draw Suzie's eyes, nose, and lips with the fabric marker. Use the medium paintbrush to paint her eyes white and her lips red. When this paint is dry, use the fine paintbrush to paint blue irises and black pupils and eyelashes.

4 To make Suzie's hair, use 40 strands of yellow yarn, each 25 inches (64 cm) long. Lay out the strands evenly and tie them together in the middle with a piece of yarn.

5 Thread the embroidery needle with a long piece of yarn and knot the end. Place the hair onto Suzie's head and sew it to the T-shirt with stitches at the top and on each side. Hold the hair in pigtails with barrettes.

HANDY HINT

To keep Hairdo Suzie's golden locks in good condition, this T-shirt should be washed by hand and laid flat to dry. Do not forget to remove Suzie's barrettes and ribbons before washing the T-shirt.

Busy Executive

When is a T-shirt not a T-shirt? When it is painted to look like an executive's shirt and tie. Decorating a plain T-shirt to look like other kinds of clothing is easy. You could paint a police officer's jacket and include details, such as a badge and a whistle. Or you could paint a doctor's coat complete with a stethoscope. There is no limit to the costumes you can make!

YOU WILL NEED

- Large piece of cardboard
- Long-sleeved white T-shirt
- Fabric marker
- Cup of water
- Fabric paints (light and dark blue, black, orange, white, red, gold)
- Fine and medium paintbrushes

1 Place pieces of cardboard inside the body and sleeves of the T-shirt. Use the fabric marker to draw the outlines of the collar, tie, buttons, and pocket on the front of the T-shirt. Draw a watch at the end of one sleeve.

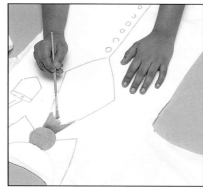

2 Use the medium paintbrush to paint the tie with light blue fabric paint. Add dark blue paint just under the knot of the tie so it stands out. When the blue paint is dry, decorate the tie with dots of orange fabric paint.

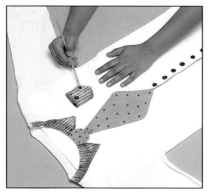

3 Paint buttons down the front of the shirt with dark blue fabric paint. Use light blue fabric paint for the collar and the pocket. Let this paint dry before painting dark blue stripes on the collar and the pocket. Paint a button on the pocket, too.

4 Mix white and black fabric paints to make gray. Paint the face of the watch gray. When the gray paint is dry, paint a red outline and black hands. To make the watch look valuable, paint the watchband with gold fabric paint.

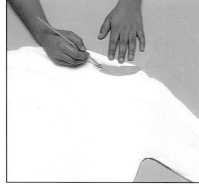

5 When the paint is dry, turn the T-shirt over, making sure the cardboard stays in place. Use the fabric marker to draw the outline of the collar on the back of the T-shirt. Paint the collar as in step 3, then draw and paint the rest of the watchband.

HANDY HINT

Copy pictures of businesspeople, police officers, and doctors from magazines so your T-shirt designs will be accurate. Colored pictures will make it easy for you to choose exactly the right colors.

Tic-tac-toe

This T-shirt is a lot of fun! It is not often that a piece of clothing can double as a game, is it?
If you wear it when you are traveling long distances, you will never be bored.
Before washing this T-shirt, remove the Xs and Os.

YOU WILL NEED

- 2 pieces of cardboard
- Short-sleeved T-shirt
- Ruler
- Fabric marker
- Pearl fabric paint (orange)
- Pencil
- Tracing paper
- Paper
- Scissors
- Blue and red felt
- Fabric glue and brush
- 9 pairs of self-adhesive Velcro dots

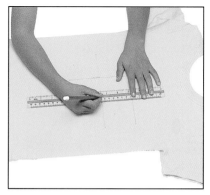

1 Place a piece of cardboard inside the body of the T-shirt. Use the ruler and the fabric marker to measure and draw the tic-tac-toe grid. The lines of the grid should be 10 inches (25 cm) long and 3 inches (8 cm) apart.

2 Paint over the grid lines with orange pearl fabric paint in a tube or a squeeze bottle. Move the tube or bottle smoothly and evenly along the lines to keep the paint from forming blobs. Let the paint dry thoroughly.

3 Make the X and O templates on page 11. Place the templates on the felt and draw around them. Make four blue Xs and four red Os. Cut out the Xs and Os. Also cut out four small, blue ovals and attach them to the centers of the Os with fabric glue.

4 Remove the protective backings from the scratchy Velcro dots. Stick one dot onto the back of each X and each O.

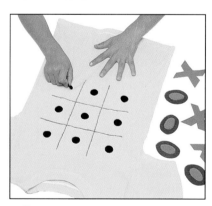

5 Remove the backings from the soft Velcro dots. Stick one dot into the center of each square on the grid. You are ready to play tic-tac-toe!

Pizza Pizzazz

This T-shirt is the ultimate in takeout food. Wherever you go, you can take your pizza with you! This mushroom and tomato pizza is just the first course. Why not make a sausage pizza, too?

YOU WILL NEED

- 2 pieces of cardboard
- Short-sleeved, light-colored T-shirt
- Plate
- Fabric marker
- Cup of water
- Fabric paint (red)
- Thick paintbrush
- Pearl fabric paint (gold)
- Pencil
- Tracing paper
- Scissors
- Brown, light brown, and red felt
- Fabric glue and brush
- 10 pairs of self-adhesive Velcro dots

1 Place a piece of cardboard inside the body of the T-shirt. Lay a medium-sized plate in the center of the T-shirt and draw around it with the fabric marker to make the pizza crust.

2 Use the thick paintbrush to cover the crust with tomato-red fabric paint. When the red paint is dry, paint the edge of the crust with gold pearl fabric paint. This pizza is looking delicious!

3 Make the mushroom and tomato templates on page 12. Place the mushroom template on the felt and draw around it. Make five whole brown mushrooms and five light brown mushroom caps. Cut out the pieces and attach the mushroom caps to the whole mushrooms with fabric glue.

4 Place the tomato template on red felt and draw around it. Make five whole tomatoes and ten tomato segments. Cut out the pieces and attach the segments to the whole tomatoes with fabric glue. Use gold pearl fabric paint to paint on seeds.

5 Remove the backings from the Velcro dots. Stick five soft dots around the edge of the pizza and stick one scratchy dot on the back of each mushroom and tomato. What would you like — a mushroom pizza or a tomato pizza?

HANDY HINT

If you cannot find Velcro dots with self-adhesive backing, you can use fabric glue to stick the dots to the T-shirt and to the felt shapes. Remove the felt shapes before washing this T-shirt.

Really Wild

It is time to go on safari, but you must tread softly so the kings of the jungle do not see you! Majestic lions and ferocious tigers might not like human impersonators prowling around in their territory.

YOU WILL NEED
- Large piece of cardboard
- Long-sleeved, light-colored T-shirt
- Fabric marker
- Cup of water
- Fabric paints (brown, red, orange, yellow, black)
- Thick paintbrush

1 Place a piece of cardboard inside the body of the T-shirt. Use the fabric marker to draw the outlines of tiger stripes on the front of the T-shirt.

2 Paint the stripes with brown, red, orange, yellow, and black fabric paints. Do not worry if the stripes are uneven. Uneven texture will make them look more realistic.

3 When the paint is dry, turn the T-shirt over. Make sure the cardboard stays in place. Use the fabric marker to draw more stripes and a tail on the back of the T-shirt.

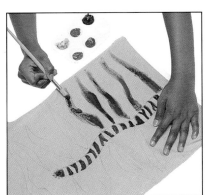

4 Use the same colors as in step 2 to paint the stripes and tail. Let the paint dry thoroughly before you start prowling and growling in your T-shirt.

Glitzy Stars

This twinkling T-shirt is perfect for a party or another special occasion. Glitter and sequins make the stars sparkle under lights. Ordinary glitter should not be used for this design. Glitter that is specially made for use on fabrics can be bought at hobby or craft shops.

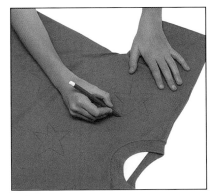

1 Place a piece of cardboard inside the body of the T-shirt. Use the fabric marker to draw the outlines of stars all over the front of the T-shirt.

2 Use the fine paintbrush to paint the stars with blue, green, red, yellow, and pink fabric paints. To make lighter shades of these colors, add white.

3 When the painted stars are dry, outline the edges with yellow pearl and gold glitter fabric paints. Decorate the stars with dots and spots of yellow and gold.

4 Now you can really add sparkle to this T-shirt. Paint your decorated stars with fabric glue. While the glue is still wet, sprinkle on fabric glitter and sequins. Then let the glue dry.

5 You can remove excess fabric glitter and sequins by gently shaking the T-shirt over the piece of paper. Carefully fold the paper to form a spout and pour the glitter and sequins back into their containers.

All-weather T-shirt

This T-shirt can be designed to match any weather forecast — except, perhaps, gale-force winds. If rain is coming, paint a rainbow on the back and flashes of lightning on the front. The perfect winter T-shirt could be covered with snowflakes.

YOU WILL NEED

- Large piece of cardboard
- Long-sleeved light blue T-shirt
- Plate
- Fabric marker
- Cup of water
- Fabric paints (yellow, red, white)
- Medium and thick paintbrushes
- Sponge

HANDY HINT

To make the clouds light and wispy, do not load too much paint on the sponge. To get the interesting texture of the sponge, press it gently onto the T-shirt.

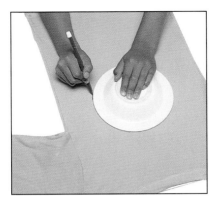

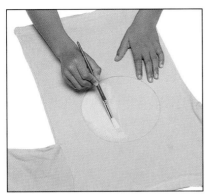

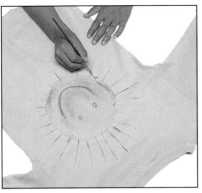

1 Place pieces of cardboard inside the body and sleeves of the T-shirt. Lay a medium-sized plate on the back of the T-shirt and draw around it with the fabric marker.

2 Use the thick paintbrush to paint this circle with sunny yellow fabric paint. When the paint is dry, use the fabric marker to give the sun a smiling face and lots of rays.

3 Mix red and yellow fabric paints to paint the eyes, mouth, and sun rays different shades of orange.

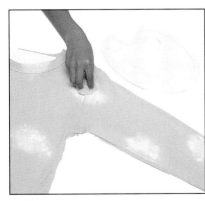

4 When the paint is completely dry, turn the T-shirt over. Make sure the cardboard stays in place. Lightly dip the dry sponge into white fabric paint.

5 Dab the sponge on the front of the T-shirt to make a wispy cloud. Repeat this step until the front and sleeves of the T-shirt are covered with clouds. Let the paint dry.

Birthday Present

Why not make this T-shirt as a gift for a friend's birthday? Your friend could wear it to his or her own party! It is important that the painted ribbon match the real ribbon. To do this, you might have to combine fabric paints to make exactly the right color.

- Large piece of cardboard
- Short-sleeved T-shirt
- Ruler
- Fabric marker
- Cup of water
- Fabric paints (green, white, pink)
- Medium and thick paintbrushes
- 15-20 inches (38-50 cm) of wide, green ribbon
- Scissors
- Green thread
- Needle

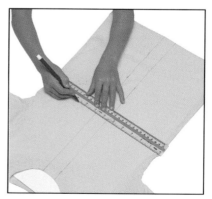

1 Place pieces of cardboard inside the body and sleeves of the T-shirt. Use the ruler and the fabric marker to draw parallel lines; two down the center of the T-shirt and two across the T-shirt.

2 Use the thick paintbrush to paint the area inside the lines with green fabric paint. Keep the edges as straight as possible. These painted stripes are the ribbons on the present. Let the paint dry.

3 Use the medium paintbrush to decorate the painted ribbon with small dots of white fabric paint. Wash the brush. Then cover the rest of the T-shirt with large pink dots. Let the paints dry thoroughly.

4 Tie the real ribbon into a big bow and trim the ends. Thread the needle and tie a knot in the end of the thread. Position the bow where the painted ribbons cross and sew it securely in place.

HANDY HINT

Adding a little water to fabric paint makes the paint easier to apply and changes the color slightly. The more water you add, the lighter the color will become. Do not make the paint too runny, or it will drip everywhere.

Hungry Cat

This hungry cat is dreaming of a seafood feast. If the dream does not come true, the cat's contented purr will become a moaning meow. Does the cat get its wish? Look at the back of the T-shirt to find out. Oh, dear, poor little fish!

YOU WILL NEED

- 2 pieces of cardboard
- Short-sleeved T-shirt
- Pencil
- Tracing paper
- Scissors
- Fabric marker
- Cup of water
- Fabric paints (blue, white, black, red, yellow, orange, pink)
- Medium and thick paintbrushes
- Sponge
- Black embroidery floss
- Embroidery needle

1 Place a piece of cardboard inside the body of the T-shirt. Make the cat template on page 12. Lay the template on the front of the T-shirt and draw around it with the fabric marker.

2 Use the thick paintbrush to paint the cat's face with blue-gray fabric paint. To make this paint color, mix blue, white, and black. Add more white to this color to paint the cat's markings.

3 Draw five fish with the fabric marker. Paint each fish a different color. This hungry cat is dreaming of a seafood supper, so give it a happy, contented face. Paint and decorate the cat's fancy collar.

4 Make the fish skeleton stencil on page 13. When the fabric paint on the front is dry, turn the T-shirt over. Place the stencil on the back of the T-shirt and dab it with a sponge dipped in red fabric paint. Lift off the stencil. Then stencil four more skeletons in different colors.

5 When the fabric paint is completely dry, turn the T-shirt over again and remove the cardboard from inside. Thread the needle with black embroidery floss and tie a knot at the end. Sew four long stitches on each side of the cat's nose to make its whiskers.

Sunny Sunflower

On this bright T-shirt, you can show off all your artistic flair for color, texture, and shape. In fact, your painting will be so good it will be framed in gold. Only one thing is missing from this painting — the signature of the talented artist.

YOU WILL NEED

- Large piece of cardboard
- Short-sleeved white T-shirt
- Fabric marker
- Cup of water
- Medium paintbrush
- Fabric paints (black, yellow, red, orange, light blue, gold)
- Glitter fabric paint (gold)

1 Place a piece of cardboard inside the body of the T-shirt. Use the fabric marker to draw the outlines of the sunflower and the fancy picture frame.

2 Paint the center of the sunflower with black fabric paint. Use shades of yellow, red, and orange to paint the petals. Let the paint dry thoroughly.

3 Use light blue fabric paint for the background of your sunflower painting. Be careful not to paint over the petals or into the frame. Let the paint dry thoroughly.

4 With a clean paintbrush, paint the picture frame with gold fabric paint. For the final artistic touch, decorate the gold frame with swirls of gold glitter fabric paint.

HANDY HINT

If you splash fabric paint on your clothes, soak them immediately in lots of cold water. Keep rinsing them until the fabric paint stain is gone. Then wash the clothes in warm, soapy water.

Glossary

barrette: a decorative clip or fastener that holds hair in place.

dab: to press lightly or pat quickly and gently.

design: (n) the arrangement of lines, shapes, colors, and patterns that form a work of art.

dye: (n) a coloring agent; a substance that, when dissolved in a liquid, such as water, will transfer some of its coloring to another material, such as cloth, hair, or leather.

embroidery: decorative stitching on fabrics, done with needles and threads, by hand or machine.

features: the individual parts of the face, such as mouth, nose, eyes, and eyebrows.

felt: (n) a thick, heavy fabric made by heating and pressing together, rather than weaving, wool and other fibers.

fluorescent: bright and glowing.

masking tape: a papery-textured tape with sticky, adhesive backing that can be used for many different purposes, such as protecting surfaces when painting near or around them.

nozzle: a short, narrow tube that tapers to a point, which can be used to direct the flow of liquids, such as water and paint.

parallel: going in the same direction and always the same distance apart, without ever meeting.

secure: (v) to tie or fasten firmly.

seeping: slowly leaking or soaking through pores or small openings.

segment: a separate and distinct part or section into which something can be divided.

sequins: small, usually flat, circle-shaped pieces of glittery metal or plastic used for decoration, especially on clothing and fashion accessories.

spiral: a line that circles or winds around a central point, forming a coil.

splatter painting: an artistic technique in which droplets of paint are scattered over a surface by flicking the paint from the bristles of a brush.

squeamish: overly sensitive or easily offended.

stencil: a sheet of stiff material with a design cut into it, over which ink or paint is spread to transfer the design onto a surface or material beneath it.

template: a flat, usually stiff, piece of material with a particular shape that, when outlined, transfers that identical shape onto another surface or material.

texture: the look or feel of a material or substance.

tutti-frutti: a sweet food, such as ice cream, that contains pieces of chopped mixed fruits, usually candied, or a mixture of fruit flavors.

More Books To Read

Costume Crafts. Worldwide Crafts (series). Iain MacLeod-Brudenell (Gareth Stevens)

Decorating T-Shirts. How to Make (series). Ray Gibson (EDC)

The Dressing-up Book: Lots of Ideas for Amazing Hats, Masks, and Costumes. Jump! Activity (series). Wendy Baker, et al (World Book, Inc.)

Fabric Fun for Kids: Step-by-Step Projects for Children (and Their Grown-ups). Julie Bates Dock (Now & Then)

Fabric Painting Funstation. Melanie Williams (Price Stearn Sloan)

Jazz Up Your Jeans: Tips and Tricks To Wake Up Your Wardrobe. Brooks Whitney (Pleasant Company)

The Most Excellent Book of Dress Up. Moe Casey (Copper Beech Books)

Stencil Fun Kid Kit. Usborne Books and Ray Gibson (EDC)

T-Shirts. How It's Made (series). Arlene Erlbach (Lerner)

Videos

Crafts for Kids. (Kids Core)

Decorative Craft Painting. (Morris Video)

Dip and Tie Dye. Kids 'n' Crafts (series). (Morris Video)

Fun with Paints. (Do It Yourself, Inc.)

Introduction to Creative Fabric Painting. (Victorian Video Productions)

Textiles. (Barr Media Group)

Web Sites

www.family.go.com/Features/family_1999_05/famf/famf59splatter/famf59splatter.html

www.azfamily.com/kids/crafts/handshirt.html

Due to the dynamic nature of the Internet, some web sites stay current longer than others. To find additional web sites, use a reliable search engine with one or more of the following keywords: *art, costumes, crafts, fabric painting, fashions, stencils,* and *T-shirts.*

Index